Stock Market Shopping: Buy Like Vegetables, Earn Like Gold!

--- Learn to invest by doing what you already know best – shopping smart.

"Dream big. Plan well. Shop smart. Earn richly."

SABAREESWARAN.B

(Working professional, Self Learner & Wealth Builder)

Dedication

> To my loving wife and little daughter.
>
> While I was busy writing this book, you both gave up a lot.
> My wife managed everything at home — cooking, cleaning,
> and taking care of everything on her own.
> My daughter missed spending time with me, yet never
> complained.
>
> Thank you both for your love, patience, and support.
> This book is for you.

My Readers:

Follow me on YouTube: **@Fintalkz_Sabari**

Follow me on Instagram: **_fintalkz**

For Training / Workshop: **fintalkz24@gmail.com**

Preface

This book was written for the everyday person — the homemaker, the college student, the middle-class employee — who wants to invest but feels overwhelmed.

For years, I noticed how people shop with great care when buying vegetables or groceries, comparing prices, checking freshness, and deciding based on daily needs. Yet, when it comes to investing — something far more impactful — many either guess or avoid it altogether.

That got me thinking: What if we approached stocks like we approach shopping?
Could the same principles apply? The answer is yes — and that's how this book was born.

In these pages, you'll find analogies, real-life comparisons, and simple principles that make stock investing feel less like rocket science and more like daily decision-making.

My goal is to help you see the stock market as a familiar place — not a battlefield — and empower you to invest smartly and calmly.

Acknowledgement

I am deeply grateful to my family, especially my wife and daughter, whose support and belief in me gave me the strength to write this book.

To the many friends, mentors, and fellow investors who shared insights and stories — thank you. Your experiences shaped the analogies and examples used throughout.

A special thanks to all the readers who will pick up this book — may it guide you to invest wisely and live prosperously.

Prologue

Imagine this..

You walk into your local market to buy vegetables. You scan the stalls, compare prices, check the quality, and maybe even haggle a little. You don't buy just anything — you buy what makes sense for your needs, your budget, and your future meals.

Now imagine doing the same with stocks.

The truth is, the mind-set you use while shopping — being alert, comparing options, understanding value — is the very same mind-set that can make you a successful investor.

This book bridges the gap between your everyday decisions and your financial future. Through simple comparisons, practical logic, and an everyday shopper's perspective, you'll learn to "buy like vegetables" and — if you do it right — "earn like gold."

Let's begin.

About the Author

Hi, I'm **Sabareeswaran.B** graduated in **B.Tech Information Technology** — a full-time Working Professional, Self Learner and a part-time Wealth Builder. For the last **13+ years**, I've been involved in:

- Equity trading, swing trading, and intraday
- Futures, options, crypto & forex
- Mutual fund investing and long-term wealth planning
- Technical and fundamental analysis
- Free mentorship for anyone who asks investment advice
- YouTube content creation to share simple financial knowledge

"Wait... how do I manage this with a full-time job?"

Well, I've learned to balance both. I work in a multinational company, but **my passion lies in helping others become financially independent** — especially women, students, and working professionals. I used to manage stock activities after work hours, during long travels, weekends and grew wealth while maintaining a 9-to-6 job without compromise. At the same time I haven't compromised on spending time with my wife and my little princes.

I'm not a SEBI registered advisor — this book is from experience, not for tips.

When I started, **there were no smartphones, no low-cost internet**. I used to pay **₹200 for just 1 GB** of data to access stock market information!

Today, you get **1.5 GB per day for the same price**, but it's spent mostly on entertainment and social media. Most people today spend hours scrolling through reels and posts. Why not spend 15 minutes a day looking at stocks instead?

- Learn a little
- Invest a little
- Grow a lot

Whether you're a college student, a new mom, or a working woman — you can build wealth in your free time, on your phone, in your own way.

Because **you already run your home like a CFO (Chief Finance Officer)**

It's time to run your investments too.

I say — let's use it wisely.

- Spend 30 minutes a day on learning stocks.
- Within 3–5 years, you'll see a whole new financial version of yourself.

This book is not written for experts. It's written for you —the homemaker, the student, the side hustler... who wants more from life.

I assure 110% that this book will not have any chart representations or complex data structures. It is purely designed by my own experience after struggling in many situations with a simple story telling format.

Without proper guidance I lost money, lost emotions, had many sleepless nights but never lost confidence and my learning's which have brought me here to write a wonderful book for you.

Definitely my presence in your life through this book will be an eye opener for how simple it is to invest in the stock market to grow wealth.

Let's **shop for stocks** like vegetables — and **watch your money grow like gold.** Ready to learn how *price fluctuation is like tomato prices?*

Let's begin this new journey: **"Stock Market Shopping: Buy Like Vegetables, Earn Like Gold"**

Contents

A Little Curiosity & Success Stories — 1

Part 1: From Kitchen to Cash – Why Women & Students Should Invest

1. **Why Every Woman Should Be a Wealth Creator** — 8
   - Radha & Meena's Real-Life Investment Journey
   - Small Steps, Big Dreams – Start with ₹1000/month
   - Turning Groceries into Gold – Invest in What You Use
   - Students Too: Cars, Business, and Dream Homes

2. **Your First Money Goal – How Much, How Soon & How Realistic** — 13
   - Why Goals Matter (Not Just Dreams)
   - Choosing a Goal That Excites You
   - Setting a Realistic Time Frame
   - Doing the Easy Math (Monthly & Weekly Breakdown)
   - Visualizing & Emotionally Connecting with Your Goal

Part 2: Stock Market = Vegetable Bazaar

3. Welcome to the Stock Bazaar   **19**
- What Is the Stock Market?
- How It Works – The Daily Market Analogy
- Who Sells and Who Buys – Role of Companies and Investors

4. Price Fluctuation – Just Like Tomatoes!   **21**
- What Makes Stock Prices Go Up and Down
- Demand, Supply & News – Market Mood Swings
- Real-Life Comparison: Onion Price vs. Stock Volatility

5. Seasonal vs. Staple – Types of Stocks   **23**
- Defensive Stocks (Daily Use)
- Cyclical Stocks (Occasional Use)
- Finding Stability in Your Portfolio Basket

Part 3: Smart Shopping = Smart Investing

6. How to Pick Fresh Stocks Like Fresh Vegetables   **27**
- Quality Check: How to Know a Good Stock
- Avoiding Rotten Picks – Warning Signs

7. **Don't Fall for Discounted Stocks**   29
   - Penny Stocks vs. Blue-Chip Stocks
   - Are You Buying Value or Just Cheap?

8. **Buy in Kilos, Not Packets – Invest in Portions** 31
   - The SIP Way – Monthly Small Investments
   - Power of Compounding – Like Growing Curry Leaves at Home

Part 4: Budgeting Like a Pro Homemaker

9. **Budget Before You Shop (or Invest)**   35
   - Creating a Simple Financial Plan
   - The Emergency Jar – Why You Must Save First

10. **Emergency Fund 101 – Why Every Woman Needs One**   37
   - What Is an Emergency Fund
   - Real-Life Emergencies It Protects You From
   - How Much to Save & Where
   - Tips for Non-Earners – Saving from Gifts or Side Hustles

11. The Simple Art of Budgeting   **42**

- The 50:30:20 Rule
- No-Excel Budgeting Tools
- Budgeting Habits That Stick

Part 5: Your Investment Thali – A Balanced Portfolio

12. Your Investment Thali – Balanced Is Beautiful   **47**

- Diversifying with Large, Mid & Small Cap Stocks
- Thali Concept – Every Item Has a Role

13. Portfolio – Your Kitchen for a Lifetime   **49**

- Core vs Satellite Portfolio
- Avoid Overstuffing – Limit Holdings
- Dividends = Freebies – Love the Extra Lemons

14. Learn from Real Kitchens – Stories of Women & Students   **51**

- Homemaker, Student & Small Group Investing
- Start Your Investing Club – 3 Friends, 1 Goal

Part 6: Mind-set = Masala of Money

15. Control Your Emotions – Don't Let Fear or Greed Shop for You!   55
- Fear & Greed – The Two Spices to Watch
- Stick to Your Recipe – Follow Your Plan

16. Flip the Fear – Face it, Fix it, Financially   57
- Common Fears About Investing
- Myths Busted with Real Stories

Part 7: Daily Market = Daily Kitchen

17. How Rain Affects Vegetables and Stocks   61
- How News, Budgets & Elections Impact Your Money

18. Buy Trusted Brands – Not Every Stall Is Reliable   64
- Stick to Known Companies
- Research Before You Buy

19. When to Change Vendors – Exit Bad Stocks   68
- Knowing When to Sell
- How to Review Your Portfolio

Part 8: Practice Before You Cook

20. Taste Before You Buy – Try Paper Trading 72
- Learn Through Simulations
- Mistakes You Can Learn From Without Losing Money

21. Maintain a Simple Investment Diary 74
- Track Like Household Expenses
- Review and Adjust Every Month

Part 9: Speak the Market's Language – But Simple Style

22. Stock Market Made Simple 78
- What Is a Stock?
- IPO = Grand Opening
- Shares vs. Equity

23. Bull & Bear – Meet the Mood Swings of the Market 81

24. Dividends, Mutual Funds & Brokers Explained Simple Style 83
- Mutual Fund = Investment Tiffin Box

- Broker = Your Middleman
- Dividend = Bonus Lemons

25. Demat, Nifty, Sensex & Portfolio Terms   86
- Your Digital Locker
- Sensex = Market Fitness Score

26. Cheat Sheet – Market Terms in Kitchen & Street Lingo   87

Part 10: Tiny Habits, Big Wealth

27. One Daily Habit That Builds Financial Smarts   94
- 5-Minute Daily Ritual
- Daily Tracker
- Affirmations & Visuals

28. Why It Works – Brain Science Behind Tiny Habits   96
- You Grow Without Realizing
- 30-Day Practice Challenge

Part 11: Your First Investment Recipe – A Step-by-Step Action Plan   99

A LITTLE CURIOSITY & SUCCESS STORIES

Before We Begin…

Is this book for you?

Yes!

Whether you are:

- ❖ a housewife who runs her home and shops for vegetables
- ❖ a student who saves from pocket money
- ❖ or someone who has never heard the word "stock"…

This book is made **just for you**.

Simple Questions You May Have!

☹ **"I don't understand shares. Can I still learn?"**

Yes. If you've ever gone shopping for vegetables, you already know the basics! You know what to buy, when to buy, and how much to pay. The stock market is similar — here, we buy *shares of companies* instead of vegetables.

☹ **"Is it risky?"**

Even buying vegetables can go wrong. Sometimes, tomatoes rot the next day. But with experience, you learn how to pick good ones. Same with stocks — you will learn how to choose safely.

☹ **"How much money do I need to start?"**
Less than your daily shopping money! You can begin with just ₹100.

A Little Curiosity for You!

Imagine this:

You go to the local vegetable market — the *sabzi mandi*. You pick fresh tomatoes, potatoes, and onions.

You carefully check for freshness, ask for the price and maybe even negotiate a little. You don't buy everything. You choose wisely.

Now... what if I told you that **investing in the stock market is just like vegetable shopping**?

Sounds funny? But it's true!

"	Some companies are like **onions** — always in demand.

"	Some stocks go **bad quickly**, like **brinjals in summer**.

"	And some — like **turmeric or garlic** — stay valuable for **years** if stored right.

Just like you don't blindly pick every vegetable from the shop, you shouldn't pick every stock in the market.

And here's the most exciting part —

two women, Radha and Meena, invested just ₹1,000 each per month in stocks of daily-use companies like **HUL, Britannia, Colgate**...

After **5 years**: their savings helped in paying for their kids' school fees.

After **10 years**: they bought gold for their daughters' weddings.

After **15 years**: one of them even built a house in her hometown!

All because Radha and Meena treated the **stock market like their vegetable shopping** — careful, smart, and regular.

Now think about this...

If you know when tomatoes are overpriced, or when onions are at their best rate...

If you know how to plan groceries for the month...

If you have managed monthly budgets, school fees, medical expenses, and still saved ₹500...

You are already 80% ready to become a successful investor!

You already know how to manage your home.

Now it's time to learn how to **manage and grow your money**.

This book will show you exactly how they did it — in simple language, with real stories, and step-by-step guidance.

Real-Life Success Stories

Radha (Housewife)

Radha started with just ₹500 per month in 2008. She invested in a simple company she uses every day — **Hindustan Unilever (HUL).**

- HUL share price in 2008: ₹250
- Share price in 2023: ₹2,500
- Investment growth in 15 years: **10x (₹500/month became over ₹1,50,000)**

Radha used the money to pay for her daughter's college education and later bought a gold chain for her daughter's wedding — all from stock savings!

> *"I never thought buying shares was this simple. It's just like buying rice and vegetables — know what you need, and buy at the right time."*

Meena (College Student)

Meena saved birthday money and part-time job income. In 2015, she bought shares of **Asian Paints** with ₹5,000.

- Asian Paints in 2015: ₹800
- Asian Paints in 2023: ₹3,200
- Returns in 8 years: **4x (₹5,000 became ₹20,000)**

She continued investing regularly. Today, her portfolio is worth **₹1.2 lakhs**.

She used part of the money to:

- Start a small T-shirt business online
- Buy a used bike
- Save for her dream to build a home for her parents

"My friends spent their savings on shopping. I invested in a company that paints houses — now my dream is to paint one for my family!"

Here's how their money quietly grew:

They didn't trade daily.

They didn't look at charts.

They just followed three golden rules:

- ☑ **Invest in what you use daily** — like sugar, atta, tea powder
- ☑ **Stay consistent** — like monthly grocery shopping
- ☑ **Don't panic during dips** — treat them like discounts!

They didn't change their lifestyle.

They changed their *thinking*.

Now it's **your turn** to grow wealth without stress, fear, or financial background.

This book will help you:

- Understand how to pick safe, daily-use companies (just like selecting fresh vegetables)

- Build simple monthly habits (just like groceries!)
- And let your money grow while you take care of family, studies, or work.

Because if you can manage a kitchen budget, **you already have what it takes to be a great investor.**

One Last Thought Before You Begin...

You don't need:
- ☒ Fancy English
- ☒ High salary
- ☒ Finance degree

You only need:
- ☑ Curiosity
- ☑ Common sense
- ☑ Small savings every month

Just like how you pick:
- Fresh vegetables from the market
- Quality rice from the store
- Daily groceries at the best price

...you'll learn how to pick the **right companies** from the stock market and grow your money safely.

Part 1: From Kitchen to Cash – Why Women & Students Should Invest

Welcome to the very beginning of your empowering money journey!

Before we learn about markets or mutual funds, let's begin right where you already shine — your **kitchen shelves**, your **budget notebook**, or even your **college canteen calculations**.

In this part, we'll explore:

- Why **women and students** make natural investors
- How your daily money smarts — budgeting, planning, saving — are already half the battle won
- Real-life stories that show how small savings can grow into something big
- And most importantly, **why you should invest —** not later, but now!

You don't need a finance degree.

You just need a **pinch of curiosity**, a **spoonful of confidence**, and the belief that you **can grow your money — your way**. Let's take that first step — from the familiar warmth of your kitchen... straight into a world of financial freedom.

1

Why Every Woman Should Be a Wealth Creator

RADHA & MEENA'S REAL-LIFE INVESTMENT JOURNEY

Imagine this...

You've just returned from your monthly grocery run. The kitchen is stocked — rice, oil, atta, tea powder, and of course, those biscuits the kids love. You've cross-checked your list, compared prices across stores, and stayed perfectly within budget. That's skill.

Now, here's a thought:

What if those same skills could help grow your money quietly in the background — while you continue managing your home or studies?

Yes, **you can be a wealth creator.**

Let's begin with a story that could be yours.

Radha and Meena were neighbours from a small town. Both homemakers. Experts at balancing the household budget. One weekend, they attended a basic stock market awareness session at their local community centre.

The speaker said something powerful:

"If you can run a home, you can run an investment plan."

That struck a chord.

That very day, they began investing ₹1,000 per month through SIPs (Systematic Investment Plans), in companies they used daily — **Britannia, HUL, ITC.**

They weren't reading finance papers.

They didn't track market charts.

They just followed **three simple steps**:

✓ Invest in companies whose products they already used

✓ Do it monthly — just like grocery shopping

✓ Stay calm — even when prices dipped (discounts happen!)

Here's how their patience paid off:

Years	Total Investment	Approx. Value @15% CAGR	Used For
5 years	₹60,000	₹1,15,000+	Paid school fees
10 years	₹1,20,000	₹3,30,000+	Bought gold for daughters
15 years	₹1,80,000	₹8,10,000+	Built their small home

They didn't earn more.

They didn't cut expenses.

They simply made their savings smarter.

SMALL STEPS, BIG DREAMS – START WITH ₹1,000/MONTH

Think investing is tough?

Start like Radha and Meena — with just **₹1,000 per month**.

That's equal to:

- Two family dinners at a restaurant
- One branded pair of sandals
- A few non-essential grocery items

Here's the magic of small amounts:

Invest ₹1,000 monthly for 10 years = ₹1,20,000 invested.

At just 15% average returns, it can grow to over **₹3.3 lakh**.

You don't need a finance degree.

Just the discipline you already apply when shopping for your home.

TURNING GROCERIES INTO GOLD – INVEST IN WHAT YOU USE

Open your kitchen. Peek inside your shelves. You'll probably see:

- **Colgate** for toothpaste
- **Britannia** biscuits
- **Tata Salt**, **Aashirvaad Atta**, **Sunfeast**, **Surf Excel**

Guess what?

All of these brands are part of **listed companies**.

You already spend money on them.

Now, start **earning** from them by becoming a small shareholder.

Even if you can't buy a factory, you can own **a tiny piece** of the company through shares or mutual funds.

And as these companies grow, **so does your wealth.**

STUDENTS TOO: CARS, BUSINESS, AND DREAM HOMES

This isn't just for homemakers. Students and young professionals are also taking charge.

- **A college student** saved ₹500/month from his part-time job.
  In 5 years, he bought his first second-hand car — all from stock returns.

- **A baking enthusiast** invested during her B.Com degree.

  In 6 years, she used the money to launch her home bakery.
- **A young working couple** began investing early in marriage.

In just 8 years, they built their 1BHK dream home.

They didn't wait to become "rich."

They started with whatever they had. That's the secret.

FINAL THOUGHT!

You don't need to be a financial expert to build wealth.

- You already budget for groceries.
- You compare prices, plan ahead for school fees and festivals.
- You manage your home like a CEO.

Now, apply those same skills to create something bigger —

your own wealth basket.

"If you can run a home, you can run your financial future."

So...

Are you ready to take the first step toward becoming a wealth creator?

2

Your First Money Goal – How Much, How Soon & How Realistic

You walk into a supermarket without a list.

You forget why you came. You wander, pick random things, spend more, and still forget to buy atta!

That's exactly how most people treat their money.

They want "more money"... but for what?

They save a little... but with no clear purpose.

Let's fix that.

Let's give your money a **mission** — your **first financial goal**.

WHY GOALS MATTER (NOT JUST DREAMS)

Dream: "I want to travel to Europe someday."

Goal: "I want to save ₹2 lakh in 18 months for a Europe trip."

See the difference?

*"Dreams are beautiful — but **goals make them real.**"*

Radha and Meena (from Chapter 1) didn't just say, "We want a better future."

They had goals: school fees, gold for their daughters, a small home.

When you attach your money to a specific goal, you:

- Save more mindfully
- Spend less impulsively
- Stay motivated even during tough times

Whether it's a vacation, gold purchase, business idea, or emergency fund — **give your money a direction.**

CHOOSING A GOAL THAT EXCITES YOU

Here's a simple rule:

Pick a goal that gives you butterflies in your stomach.

Because saving for "just in case" feels boring.

But saving for something that lights you up? That's powerful.

Ask yourself:

- What's something I truly want in the next 1–3 years?
- What will make me smile when I finally achieve it?

Examples:

- A solo trip to your dream destination
- Gold bangles for your daughter's wedding
- Your own Activa or used car
- Equipment for your home baking business
- A new laptop for freelancing or online learning

This goal should **mean something to YOU.**

Not society. Not others. Just you.

SETTING A REALISTIC TIME FRAME

Your goal is exciting. Now, let's put a **deadline** on it.

A goal without a timeline is like a train ticket with no date —
you're going nowhere.

Be honest and practical:

- Can I save for this in 6 months?
- Or do I need 12 or 18 months?
- Do I have other big expenses coming up?

Don't rush and stress yourself.

Don't delay and lose motivation.

Tip: Start small and short — maybe a 6-month or 1-year goal.
Once you achieve it, go for bigger dreams.

DOING THE EASY MATH (MONTHLY & WEEKLY BREAKDOWN)

Let's say your goal is: **"I want ₹60,000 for a trip to Kerala next year."**

Here's the **easy math**:

- ₹60,000 ÷ 12 months = ₹5,000 per month
- ₹5,000 ÷ 4 weeks = ₹1,250 per week

  That's roughly what we spend on:
- 1 pizza + 2 coffee dates □
- One shopping spree at the mall
- A few unnecessary online orders

Now, instead of thinking "₹60,000 is too much,"

You're thinking, "Can I save ₹1,250 this week?"

That's doable.

Money becomes manageable when we **break it down** into bite-sized pieces.

You can even use a notebook or an app to track weekly savings and stay on track!

VISUALIZING & EMOTIONALLY CONNECTING WITH YOUR GOAL

Close your eyes and **imagine**:

- You're standing in Munnar, sipping hot tea, overlooking green hills.
- You're placing gold bangles on your daughter's wrist, and her eyes sparkle.
- You're switching on your laptop — your OWN laptop — to begin your freelancing journey.

Feel it. Smile. Believe it.

Now, **print a picture** of your goal. Stick it near your mirror, kitchen shelf, or study desk.

This is not silly. This is smart psychology.

Emotion + Vision = Action

When you connect emotionally with your goal, you're less likely to waste money on things you don't need.

Each rupee saved becomes a **step closer** to your dream.

FINAL THOUGHT!

Setting your first money goal is like planting your first seed. With the right care, it will grow into something beautiful and strong.

So today, grab a pen and write this down:
- ☑ What do I really want?
- ☑ How much do I need?
- ☑ When do I want it by?
- ☑ How much should I save monthly or weekly?
- ☑ Why is this goal important to me?

This isn't just about money.
It's about becoming the kind of woman who dreams, plans, and achieves.
Because…

"A woman with a goal is a woman with power."

Ready to set your first goal? Let's go!

Part 2: Stock Market = Vegetable Bazaar

Now that you're warmed up, let's take a stroll to your local sabzi mandi.

Sounds strange? Not really. Because the stock market works a lot like your daily vegetable shopping!

Prices go up and down, there are demand and supply, buyers and sellers — just like tomatoes and onions!

In this part, we'll keep things light and simple as we see how your daily market knowledge is the perfect training for understanding the stock market.

Get ready to look at money in a whole new — and totally familiar — way!

3

Welcome to the Stock Bazaar

WHAT IS THE STOCK MARKET?

Imagine you walk into a huge market.

There are stalls everywhere. People shouting prices.

Some buying potatoes. Others selling spinach.

Welcome to the **stock market** — just like that, but with **companies instead of vegetables.**

In simple words:

- Companies come to the stock market to **sell ownership** (called *shares*)
- People like you and me (called *investors*) buy those shares

When you buy a share, you're not just holding a piece of paper.

You're owning a tiny bit of a company — like owning one coriander leaf from the whole bunch!

HOW IT WORKS – THE DAILY MARKET ANALOGY

Just like in your vegetable market:

- Prices change every day
- Buyers and sellers bargain

- Some days are crowded, some days are dull

The stock market works similarly:

- A company's **share price** goes up or down depending on demand
- People trade these shares — some for profit, some for long-term savings
- The "market" opens and closes daily — like a bazaar with fixed hours

Think of it as an online version of your sabzi mandi — fast, busy, and full of activity!

WHO SELLS AND WHO BUYS – ROLE OF COMPANIES AND INVESTORS

In our stock bazaar:

- **Companies** are the sellers. They offer their shares to raise money for growth.
- **Investors** (you, me, mutual funds, big institutions) are the buyers.

Sometimes, sellers become buyers and buyers become sellers — depending on the price and timing.

It's all about opportunity and strategy.

Companies need money. Investors want returns. The stock market is where their paths meet.

4

Price Fluctuation – Just Like Tomatoes!

Ever walked into the market and asked the price of tomatoes?

One day it's ₹30/kg.

Next week? ₹80/kg!

Why? Demand and supply!

The same logic works for **stocks**.

WHAT MAKES STOCK PRICES GO UP AND DOWN

Here's what affects stock prices:

- More buyers than sellers? Price goes UP
- More sellers than buyers? Price goes DOWN

Just like when festivals come, and everyone wants paneer — price shoots up!

Stocks are no different. They move with:

- Company news
- Market trends
- Global events
- Budget announcements
- Even a tweet from a business tycoon!

DEMAND, SUPPLY & NEWS – MARKET MOOD SWINGS

The stock market is an **emotional place**.

One day it's excited.

Next day it's scared.

Just like how onion prices jump during monsoons or fall during harvest.

- Good news = buying spree = prices up
- Bad news = panic selling = prices down

The key is: **Don't panic**. Understand the mood. Then act wisely.

REAL-LIFE COMPARISON: ONION PRICE VS. STOCK VOLATILITY

Let's compare:

Item	Trigger	Price Fluctuation
Onion	Rain, storage issue, transport cost	From ₹25 to ₹100/kg
Stock	Earnings result, CEO change, market crash	From ₹100 to ₹60 or ₹140

Moral of the story: Prices **will** change. Your job is not to **predict**, but to **prepare**.

Buy smart. Hold strong. Think long-term.

5

Seasonal vs. Staple – Types of Stocks

Let's go back to our kitchen for a second.

There are two kinds of vegetables:

- Some you use daily: onions, tomatoes, chillies
- Some only in season or for special dishes: mangoes, avocados, peas

The stock market also has **daily-use stocks** and **occasional-use stocks**.

DEFENSIVE STOCKS (DAILY USE)

These are the **atta, dal, salt** of your investment kitchen.

They're always in demand — rain or shine, good or bad times.

Examples:

- FMCG companies (toothpaste, soap, biscuits)
- Pharma companies
- Utility services (electricity, gas)

They grow slowly, but they're **steady**. Perfect for peace of mind.

CYCLICAL STOCKS (OCCASIONAL USE)

These are like **mangoes** — loved, but only when the season is right.

Examples:

- Automobile companies
- Construction firms
- Travel and tourism
- Luxury brands

When the economy is booming, these stocks shine.

When there's a slowdown, they take a nap.

They give **high returns** if you buy at the right time.

FINDING STABILITY IN YOUR PORTFOLIO BASKET

Like every good cook knows:

Don't cook only with one ingredient.

Same with investing — mix both types.

- Use **defensive stocks** for safety
- Add **cyclical stocks** for growth

This way, your **portfolio basket** stays balanced — like a thali with everything on it.

FINAL THOUGHT!

The stock market may look big and scary from the outside,
But once you enter the **stock bazaar** with the eyes of a
smart homemaker,
You'll realize — it's all very familiar.
The prices, the moods, the choices... they're all things you
already understand.
You don't need to be a finance expert.
You just need to be a **curious learner** with a smart budget
and a steady heart.
Ready to build your own stock basket?
Let's do it — like we shop veggies: wisely, calmly, and with
full control.

Part 3: Smart Shopping = Smart Investing

In the last part, you discovered the magic of saving — from daily habits to dreaming big. Now that your savings jar is slowly filling up, it's time to ask: **how do I grow this money?**

Welcome to **Smart Shopping = Smart Investing**, where we take the familiar skills you already use in your kitchen or market and apply them to the world of investments.

You've already mastered the aisles of the market — choosing the best veggies, checking prices, comparing quality.

Now, imagine doing the same for your money.

Just like your **masala dabba** has haldi, jeera, and mirchi — each with its own role — your investment toolkit will also include **SIPs, mutual funds, shares**, and more.

Each one adds its own flavour to your financial growth.

In this part, you'll learn how to:

- Shop for stocks and funds like you shop for groceries
- Understand investment tools without jargon
- Mix and match SIPs and mutual funds to suit your taste and risk level. Build confidence, not confusion.

Think of it as picking the freshest tomatoes for your sambar — slow, careful, and full of heart.

Let's open the spice box of investing and start flavouring your financial future, one smart choice at a time.

6

How to Pick Fresh Stocks Like Fresh Vegetables

QUALITY CHECK: HOW TO KNOW A GOOD STOCK

When you're buying vegetables, what do you check?

- ✓ Colour
- ✓ Smell
- ✓ Firmness
- ✓ Freshness

Now apply the same logic to **stocks**.

Here's your simple **Stock Quality Checklist**:

- **Financials** – Is the company making consistent profits?
- **Management** – Do they have smart, ethical leaders?
- **Growth** – Is the company growing steadily over the years?
- **Reputation** – What do people say about it? News matters.

Good companies don't need fancy marketing — their **quality speaks** through numbers and trust.

Remember:

> A shiny brinjal on top might look tempting,
> But check what's beneath before adding it to
> your basket!

AVOIDING ROTTEN PICKS – WARNING SIGNS

Some vegetables look okay from outside but turn out to be **rotten inside**.

Stocks are the same.

Watch out for these **bad stock signs**:

- Sudden, unexplained price spikes
- Frequent CEO changes
- Heavy debts with no repayment plan
- Promoters selling their own shares
- Losses for many years in a row

If something **feels off**, it probably is.

Avoid emotional buying — don't fall for flashy stock tips from WhatsApp groups or YouTube hype.

Instead, ask:

> Would I put this in my shopping bag if I had to
> cook dinner with it?

If the answer is no, skip it.

7

Don't Fall for Discounted Stocks

PENNY STOCKS VS. BLUE-CHIP STOCKS

Imagine someone says:

"Hey! These mangoes are only ₹10 per kg!"

Tempting, right? But then you see they're half-rotten.

That's what **penny stocks** are — super cheap, but **high risk**.

Compare them to **blue-chip stocks**:

- These are like high-quality branded grains — a bit costlier, but **reliable**.
- They belong to well-established companies with a long track record.

Here's a quick view:

Type	Price	Risk	Potential
Penny Stocks	Very Low	Very High	Could go to zero or 10x
Blue-Chips	Moderate-High	Low	Steady growth over time

Sometimes, **cheap isn't value — it's just low quality**.

ARE YOU BUYING VALUE OR JUST CHEAP?

Imagine you're at the grocery store. You spot two packets of rice:

- **Packet A – ₹80**: A well-known brand, clean grains, full weight, trusted by many.
- **Packet B – ₹40**: No brand, dusty grains, half the quantity, and looks suspicious.

At first glance, Packet B seems like a bargain. But is it really? If you think long-term — quality meals, no wastage, no doctor visits from bad rice — **Packet A actually gives better value**, even though it costs more.

The same rule applies to investing.

- Just because a stock is cheap doesn't mean it's good.
- And just because it's costly doesn't mean it's bad.

Low price isn't always a "deal." High price isn't always a "trap."

- ☑ **Buy for value** — choose stocks that have strong foundations, steady growth, and long-term potential.
- ☒ **Don't fall for discounts** — avoid stocks that are cheap only because they're weak or risky.

Before buying any investment, always pause and ask: **Am I getting more than what I'm paying for — or less?**

That one question can turn you from a casual buyer into a smart investor.

8

Buy in Kilos, Not Packets – Invest in Portions

THE SIP WAY – MONTHLY SMALL INVESTMENTS

Do you buy 50 kg of onions in one day?

Of course not. You buy little by little — enough for the week.

Same way, investing should be in **small, regular amounts**.

This is called an **SIP (Systematic Investment Plan)** —

You invest a fixed amount (say ₹1,000) every month in a mutual fund or stock.

Why is this smart?

- You don't need a huge lump sum to start
- You reduce the risk of buying at a "bad time"
- You build a habit of saving and investing

Over time, your portfolio grows — **slowly but surely**.

POWER OF COMPOUNDING – LIKE GROWING CURRY LEAVES AT HOME

Think of planting curry leaves at home. At first, it's just a stem in a pot.

But you water it daily, let the sun do its magic — and weeks later, you're adding fresh leaves to your rasam.

That's **compounding** in investing:

- Your money earns returns
- Those returns also earn returns
- And the cycle continues — growing like a healthy plant

Even small amounts, if invested regularly, can turn into **big wealth** over time.

Invest ₹500/month for 20 years at 12% return?

You'll get over **₹5 lakh!**

All because of **discipline + time + compounding**.

FINAL THOUGHT!

Investing is *not* about timing the market.

It's about **staying in the market** — like a smart shopper who knows when and what to buy.

- Look for quality
- Avoid emotional traps
- Buy in small portions
- Let your money grow like a backyard curry leaf tree

You already have the instincts.

Now you're building the tools.

Ready to fill your **investment basket** with fresh, valuable picks?

Let's keep going!

Part 4: Budgeting Like a Pro Homemaker

By now, you've learned the importance of getting started, building confidence, and setting your financial kitchen in order. You've seen how saving a little can go a long way. Small jars slowly fill up, and now it's time to decide how to use them wisely.

Welcome to budgeting — the invisible thread that holds everything together.

Think of a homemaker. She isn't just cooking meals or keeping the house tidy. She is silently running a mini economy. She knows how to manage ₹100 or ₹10,000 with the same care, making every rupee count. She juggles groceries, school fees, sudden repairs, and birthday gifts — all without Excel sheets or finance degrees.

That's budgeting in action. Quiet. Practical. Powerful.

Just like you wouldn't go to the vegetable market without a list, you shouldn't go into the world of investing without a money plan. Without a list, you'll overspend, miss essentials, and regret your choices later. Budgeting is your list — it keeps you focused, clear, and in control.

In this part, you'll learn how to:

- Create simple, soulful financial plans — not scary ones
- Understand why your Emergency Jar is both an emotional and financial safety net
- Save smartly even if you don't have a salary — using gifts, side gigs, cashback, and clever cuts
- Use tools like the 50:30:20 rule, no-Excel budgeting tricks, and small habits that make a big difference

Remember, budgeting isn't about restriction. It's about freedom — knowing where your money is going and feeling confident about it .It's not a punishment. It's a preparation.

It's like meal planning. You plan meals to avoid waste, save time, and stay healthy. Budgeting does the same for your money. It gives your money a purpose and direction. Start with what you have. Even ₹100 has power when you give it a job. Label your jars: daily expenses, savings, emergencies, dreams. Watch how clarity changes your relationship with money.

Let's embrace budgeting like we embrace planning our weekly meals — with purpose, care, and confidence.

Because behind every strong kitchen is a thoughtful plan. And behind every successful investor is a wise budget.

9

Budget Before You Shop (or Invest)

CREATING A SIMPLE FINANCIAL PLAN

Before heading to the market, you check:

- What you already have
- What you need to buy
- How much you can spend

That's a **financial plan** in its simplest form.

In money terms, it means:

- Knowing your income (salary, rent, business, etc.)
- Listing your expenses (bills, groceries, travel)
- Setting aside money for savings and goals

Think of it like your **monthly menu plan**.
Without it, you'll overspend on snacks and forget to buy rice!

A good plan avoids waste — both in the kitchen and in your wallet.
It brings peace of mind, because you know where every rupee is going.

THE EMERGENCY JAR – WHY YOU MUST SAVE FIRST

Remember the "secret box" your mom or grandma kept —
filled with ₹10, ₹50 notes for "just in case"?
That's your Emergency Jar. And it's non-negotiable in
financial planning. This small stash wasn't for movie tickets
or shopping sprees .It was for doctor visits, school
emergencies, surprise guests — the uninvited expenses that
life brings without warning.

Always pay yourself first.
Before buying anything — save a portion.
Even ₹500 a month saved consistently becomes your safety
cushion in tough times. Your Emergency Jar is not for
investing or spending — it's your shield. It gives you the
freedom to breathe, the power to pause, and the peace to
stay calm when things go wrong.

You won't realise its value... until one day you need it. And
when you do, it will be your quiet hero.

"If budgeting is cooking for today,
Emergency saving is keeping something for tomorrow."

So, start small. Start now.
Your future self will thank you for every rupee you saved
with love and intention.

10

Emergency Fund 101 – Why Every Woman Needs One

WHAT IS AN EMERGENCY FUND?

An emergency fund is your personal safety net — money kept aside only for **real emergencies**, not for shopping sales, movie nights, or last-minute pizza cravings.

It's like that hidden packet of pickles or instant noodles you keep in your kitchen — not for everyday use, but for the day you run out of groceries or guests arrive without notice.

Your emergency fund steps in when life takes an unexpected turn:

- **Medical expenses** — sudden fever, hospital visits
- **Sudden travel** — urgent family matters or personal emergencies
- **Job loss** — when income stops but bills don't
- **Appliance repair** — broken fridge or geyser in winter

- **Rent delay** — to avoid awkward calls from the landlord

This fund is **not** an investment. It's not for profit.
It's **pure protection** — like an umbrella in your bag when clouds gather.

The best part?
No paperwork. No running to borrow. No stress. No guilt.
You simply reach for it — like your emergency candle during a power cut.

Start with what you can — ₹500, ₹1000 a month — and let it quietly grow in a separate account or envelope.

Remember:
Peace of mind isn't bought. It's saved.
Your emergency fund gives you control in moments you feel helpless.

It's not about how much you have —
It's about knowing you're ready, come what may.

REAL-LIFE EMERGENCIES IT PROTECTS YOU FROM

Let's say:

- Your child falls sick and needs hospital care
- Your spouse's salary is delayed this month
- Your mobile breaks and you need one urgently for work

In all these cases, you won't panic if you have an **emergency fund**.

It buys you **time, confidence, and calm**.

HOW MUCH TO SAVE & WHERE?

Here's a simple rule: Save at least **3 to 6 months' worth of expenses**

If your family spends ₹25,000/month, try to save around ₹75,000 to ₹1.5 lakhs as your fund.

Where to keep it?

- **Not** in your main bank account
- Keep it in a **separate savings account**, or
- **Liquid mutual fund** (easy to withdraw, low risk)

This is *not* money for investing — this is money for *safety*.

TIPS FOR NON-EARNERS – SAVING FROM GIFTS OR SIDE HUSTLES

You don't need a monthly salary to start saving.
Money can come from many small sources — you just need to catch it before it slips away like loose change.

Think of it like kitchen leftovers — a little rice here, a spoon of dal there — which together make a full meal.
Similarly, small money from different places can become your powerful savings.

You can start saving from:
- Birthday or festival gifts (that envelope with cash from relatives)
- Pocket money or festival bonuses
- Cash back from online shopping or digital wallets
- Side hustles like tailoring, baking, tutoring, art, or even helping someone with a small task

Even if the amount is small, **put 10%–30% of whatever you get into your emergency jar** or savings envelope.
Treat it like paying yourself first — just like we keep the first roti aside for God or a guest.

Consistency is more important than the amount.
₹50 saved every week is ₹2600 a year — all from places you usually forget.

"Saving is not about how much you earn,
It's about how regularly you put something aside — even if small."

Don't wait for a big job or a huge income.
Start now, with what you have.
A tiny seed still grows into a tree — but only if you plant it.

11

The Simple Art of Budgeting

THE 50:30:20 RULE

This is the easiest budgeting formula — think of it as a recipe for your monthly income!

Just like you divide your kitchen groceries into essentials, snacks, and festival specials, you can divide your money too.

Take your **total monthly income** — whether it's ₹5,000 or ₹50,000 — and break it down like this:

Purpose	% of Income	Example (₹30,000/month)
Needs (must-haves)	50%	₹15,000 (rent, groceries, electricity, school fees)
Wants (nice-to-haves)	30%	₹9,000 (shopping, eating out, subscriptions, treats)
Savings (your future)	20%	₹6,000 (SIP, emergency fund, gold savings, FDs)

Think of it like this:

- **Needs** are your daily roti-dal — you can't skip them.
- **Wants** are your samosas and ice cream — nice to have, but not urgent.
- **Savings** are your pickles — stored today, enjoyed tomorrow.

Why it works:

- It's simple — no complicated apps or Excel sheets.
- It's flexible — you can adjust it based on your priorities.
- It's guilt-free — you can still enjoy life while securing your future.

Even if your income changes, the rule stays the same — just adjust the portions.

Budgeting this way keeps you in control.
No last-minute panic. No guilt over spending.
And every rupee gets a purpose — just like every ingredient has a role in your kitchen.

Once you master this, you're not just handling money — you're running your financial kitchen like a pro!

NO-EXCEL BUDGETING TOOLS

Don't like Excel? No problem.

Here are **easy tools** you can use instead:

- Paper diary and colour pens
- Mobile apps like **Walnut, Money Manager, GoodBudget**
- Jar method – 3 labelled envelopes: **Needs, Wants, Saves**

Budgeting doesn't have to be digital or complicated.

Even an old-school **notebook** can work like magic if you're consistent.

BUDGETING HABITS THAT STICK

Tips to make budgeting a *lifestyle*:

- Do a **weekly money check-in** (takes 15 mins!)
- Set **reminders for bill due dates**
- Reward yourself when you hit saving targets
- Discuss the budget with family – make it a team effort
- Have a visual tracker — colour in blocks or use stickers

*"Money management is not a task — it's a **skill you grow**, like your best recipe."*

FINAL THOUGHT!

Budgeting is not about cutting joy.
It's about **directing joy** toward the things that truly matter.
With a budget:
- You know where your money goes
- You stop feeling guilty about spending
- You become **calm, confident, and prepared**

Just like a homemaker knows how to turn ₹500 into a week's worth of meals,

You too can turn your income into **freedom, strength, and security**.

Budget first. Invest next.
That's the golden rule for lifelong financial peace.

Part 5: Your Investment Thali – A Balanced Portfolio

You've now built a strong base — learning how to save, budget like a homemaker, and prepare for emergencies. Now, it's time to **plate up your wealth** with balance and beauty — welcome to **Your Investment Thali**!

Just like a perfect thali has a bit of everything — rice, dal, roti, sabzi, chutney — a good portfolio should be **diverse and well-proportioned**. Not too spicy, not too bland — just right for long-term nourishment. Investing isn't about going all in on the "hottest" trend. It's about building a plate (portfolio) that suits **your financial appetite** — one that satisfies today and sustains tomorrow.

In this part, you'll learn:

- How to **diversify like a thali** — with large, mid, and small-cap stocks
- The role of each element — core dishes vs. side dishes
- Why **dividends** are like the surprise pickle or sweet you didn't expect — but love anyway
- And real stories of women and students who built their own "money meals"

Because just like every item in your thali has a job — filling, energizing, soothing — every part of your portfolio has a purpose too.Let's serve your investment plate with thought, care, and a dash of flavour!

12

Your Investment Thali – Balanced Is Beautiful

DIVERSIFYING WITH LARGE, MID & SMALL CAP STOCKS

In a meal:

- **Rice** is safe, fills your stomach — but can't be eaten alone
- **Sabzi** adds flavour and variety
- **Pickle** is spicy, used in small amounts

Same with investing:

Stock Type	Like In Your Thali	Role in Portfolio
Large Cap	Rice/Roti	Stable, dependable
Mid Cap	Dal/Sabzi	Good growth, some risk
Small Cap	Pickle/Chutney	High risk, high reward – in small portions only

This is called **diversification** — not putting all your eggs (or veggies) in one basket.

It keeps your money safe, growing, and protected from market mood swings.

THALI CONCEPT – EVERY ITEM HAS A ROLE

Just like no thali has only sweets or only rice,

your investments too must be a mix — each item playing its part.

- **Rice (Large Cap)** – for foundation
- **Veggies (Mid Cap)** – for growth
- **Pickles (Small Cap)** – for thrill, in tiny doses
- **Sweets (FDs/Debt Funds)** – safety and calm
- **Salt (Cash/Liquid)** – quick access when needed

Balanced portfolio = **taste + nutrition + comfort**

Tip: Review your portfolio every 6–12 months.

Like changing your meal with the seasons, update your portfolio as your life evolves.

13

Portfolio – Your Kitchen for a Lifetime

CORE VS SATELLITE PORTFOLIO

Imagine your kitchen has:

- **Everyday staples** (rice, dal, atta)
- **Special items** (paneer, pasta, exotic sauces)

Same way, your portfolio can be divided into:

Type	Role	Example
Core	Long-term, steady growth	Large & mid cap stocks, Index funds
Satellite	High potential, short term	Small cap, thematic funds, IPOs

Don't fill your kitchen with only fancy foods.

Same with investing — keep a **strong core**, then add extras.

AVOID OVERSTUFFING – LIMIT HOLDINGS

Too many spices = confusing taste.
Too many stocks = messy portfolio.
Stick to:

- **10–15 quality stocks or funds**
- Know **why** you're investing in each — don't add just because someone said so!

Review every 6 months — like your kitchen shelf!

> *"It's okay to miss out on one hot tip,*
> *But it's not okay to burn your whole thali."*

DIVIDENDS = FREEBIES – LOVE THE EXTRA LEMONS

Some companies give back a **small portion of profit** to investors — called **dividends**.
Think of it as:

- Free lemon pickle with your thali
- Bonus coupon when you shop

You didn't ask for it — but you got rewarded **just for being a loyal customer**.

Dividends can be reinvested or saved.
Even if small, they build up into beautiful returns over time.

14

Learn from Real Kitchens – Stories of Women & Students

HOMEMAKER, STUDENT & SMALL GROUP INVESTING

Radha, the Homemaker:

Started SIPs of ₹1000/month. Treated it like monthly grocery.

Today, her daughter's education is fully funded — thanks to her consistent investing.

Anu, the College Student:

Saved from tutoring & online gigs.

Invested ₹500/week with friends. Now has over ₹60K at 22!

Three sisters in Chennai:

Started a kitchen club investment group — each puts ₹2000/month.

They learn together, invest together, and celebrate milestones like a family.

Moral?

*"You don't need lakhs. You need **habit + patience + consistency**."*

START YOUR INVESTING CLUB – 3 FRIENDS, 1 GOAL

Form your own **"Veggie Thali Investors Club"** — because learning is tastier when shared!

- Invite 2–4 trusted friends
- Pick a small fixed amount monthly
- Learn together — watch videos, read news
- Track progress monthly
- Celebrate small wins!

Even ₹1000 each becomes ₹36,000 a year as a group.

Together, you can share tips, laugh over mistakes, and cheer each other on.

You'll feel more responsible when others are counting on you too.

Take turns presenting what you've learned — make it fun like a potluck!

Use a simple notebook or WhatsApp group to track your joint journey.

Over time, your club can grow into a mini financial family.

"Investing alone is wise.

Investing together is empowering."

FINAL THOUGHT!

A thali isn't judged by just one item.
It's the **overall experience** — the balance, taste, and
feeling of satisfaction.
Your portfolio is the same.
Let it be:

- Nourishing
- Easy to digest
- Suitable for all seasons of life

Don't chase only returns — chase resilience.
And like every kitchen evolves,
Let your money kitchen grow with your dreams.

Because just like the **right spices make a dish
unforgettable**,
your **thoughts, emotions, and attitude** decide whether
your money journey is delightful or disastrous.

Part 6: Mind-set = Masala of Money

You've come a long way — from understanding how money works, to choosing your financial ingredients, building your investment thali, and budgeting like a pro.

Now it's time for the secret ingredient that brings it all together — your **mind-set**.

Every cook knows this truth: even with the best ingredients, the dish falls flat without the **right masala**.

In the same way, when it comes to money — your emotions are the spice mix.

- ☞ Fear when the market drops.
- ☞ Greed when it rises.
- ☞ Doubt when things feel uncertain.

This part is your **mind-set masala mix** — helping you stay calm, focused, and confident.

We'll explore:

- How to **manage fear & greed** like kitchen heat
- Why it's important to **stick to your recipe**, not follow others
- How to **flip fear into clarity** — with real-life stories

Because in your money kitchen, the right mind-set is what turns a good plan into a lasting dish.

Let's learn to season wisely — and cook with confidence.

15

Control Your Emotions – Don't Let Fear or Greed Shop for You!

FEAR & GREED – THE TWO SPICES TO WATCH

Imagine you're in a rush at the market.

One day you overbuy tomatoes because they're cheap (greed)

Another day you skip buying onions altogether because prices shot up (fear)

Both are **natural reactions**, but neither is **smart shopping**.

Same happens in investing:

Emotion	Looks Like	Results In
Fear	"Market is falling! Sell now!"	Panic selling, missing recovery
Greed	"This stock is doubling! Buy more!"	Overinvesting, big losses later

Too much fear → you never start.

Too much greed → you take unplanned risks.

Balance is the key masala. Not too spicy. Not too bland.

STICK TO YOUR RECIPE – FOLLOW YOUR PLAN

You wouldn't change your dosa recipe halfway just because
someone walks by and says,
"Add sugar, it'll taste better!" — right?

Investing works the same way.

Don't toss your financial plan just because:
- Your cousin suddenly says, "Crypto is the future!"
- A news anchor yells, "Big Market Crash Ahead!"
- Your neighbour flaunts profits from a lucky IPO

These are distractions — tempting but temporary.

Stick to what **you** planned:
- Your monthly SIPs
- Your budgeting jars
- Your emergency fund
- Your investment thali — handpicked and homemade

These are your tried-and-tested ingredients.

They may not sizzle like fast fads, but they **nourish your future**.

If your recipe is thoughtful, the outcome will be delicious —
even if it simmers slowly.

Patience cooks wealth best.

"Let your emotions be the garnish, not the chef."

16

Flip the Fear – Face It, Fix It, Financially

COMMON FEARS ABOUT INVESTING

"What if I lose all my money?"
Answer: Start small. Use SIPs. You're not buying lottery tickets; you're buying ownership in good companies.

"I don't understand finance. It's too complex."
Answer: You run a home. That's finance. If you can budget monthly groceries, you can invest smartly.

"I'll wait for the 'right time.'"
Answer: There's no perfect time. Even the best chefs cook with what's in season. Start now, even if it's with ₹500.

MYTHS BUSTED WITH REAL STORIES

Myth: "Investing is only for working women or men."
Truth: Seema, a homemaker, built a ₹5L corpus by saving her festive gifts and investing them regularly.

Myth: "I'm too young to invest."

Truth: Kavya, a 19-year-old college student, started SIPs of ₹300/month from her tuition money. In 5 years, she had more than ₹25K with compounding.

Myth: "I've missed the bus. I'm too old now."

Truth: Lakshmi aunty started at 52. By 60, her mutual fund portfolio helped her travel across India — solo!

The only thing between **you and your financial freedom** ...is a mind-set makeover.

FINAL MASALA TIP!

Every kitchen has its spice box.

Every investor has their **mind-set box**.

Keep:

- ☑ Discipline
- ☑ Patience
- ☑ Confidence
- ☑ Curiosity
- ☑ Courage (just enough!)

Avoid:

- ☒ Panic
- ☒ Peer pressure
- ☒ Overthinking

Master your money masala — and the entire financial journey becomes **your signature recipe**

Part 7: Daily Market = Daily Kitchen

Beautiful! You've come a long way.
You've mastered the financial recipes, gathered the right ingredients,
measured your portions with care, and seasoned your mindset with confidence.

Now, welcome to the final — and most empowering — part of your journey:
Daily Market = Daily Kitchen

This is where investing becomes as natural as preparing your morning chai.
It's no longer a once-in-a-while event. It's part of your daily rhythm, just like planning meals or shopping for groceries.

The market doesn't need to feel distant or difficult.
It's not just numbers on a screen or suits in a boardroom.
It's as real and relatable as your neighbourhood vegetable shop.

You already know how to:

- Compare prices
- Choose quality over quantity
- Avoid waste

- Make smart swaps based on the season

These same habits keep your **financial pantry** in order too.

Just like you wouldn't let your fridge sit idle and empty,
you shouldn't let your money stay still.

Let's see how your everyday kitchen smarts — planning,
consistency, awareness —
can keep your **investment thali** fresh, balanced, and full of
flavour every day.

It's time to stir the pot, check the heat, and keep your
financial meal cooking!

17

How Rain Affects Vegetables and Stocks

HOW NEWS, BUDGETS & ELECTIONS IMPACT YOUR MONEY

Ever noticed how a week of heavy rain can completely change the vegetable market?

It can:

- **Raise prices of tomatoes**
- **Reduce supply**
- **Make you rethink what to cook for the week**

But just like the weather, the stock market can experience sudden shifts, influenced by events in the world around us. **The stock market is just like the rain** — unpredictable, yet it affects everyone.

Rain = News. News influences how we feel, how we invest, and how we act.

Just like you wouldn't buy tomatoes at an inflated price during a storm, understanding the market's reaction to external factors can help you navigate through it calmly.

Event Type and Market Effect:

- **Budget Announcements**:
  Just as a government budget can affect the price of food,
  a national budget has a direct impact on stocks in sectors
  like banking, infrastructure, and energy. Stocks might
  rise or fall based on new policies and reforms announced.
- **Elections**:
  Elections are like unpredictable weather patterns. The
  market reacts to predictions of political stability. If
  investors expect a stable government, stocks in sectors
  like banking or infrastructure may see growth.
  Conversely, uncertainty can lead to market fluctuations.
- **Global News**:
  Just like how rain in one region can affect vegetable
  prices worldwide, global events can have a far-reaching
  impact on markets. Things like war, changes in oil prices,
  or international crises can shake the global market,
  impacting stocks even in India.

What Should You Do in These Times?

- **Stay informed, not overwhelmed**:
  Just like you keep an eye on the weather forecast to know
  when it's safe to step outside, stay updated on global and
  national news, but don't let every headline make you

panic. Understand the market's response to events, but don't react impulsively.

- **Don't panic sell**:
  Just as you wouldn't sell your kitchen vegetables in a rush during a rainstorm, don't sell off your investments at the first sign of trouble. The market might seem volatile, but selling in panic often locks in losses.
- **If you've picked quality stocks, they'll bounce back**:
  Think of it like seasonal vegetables. When the weather clears, fresh stock will return to the market. Likewise, good-quality stocks will weather the storm and recover over time. The key is to stay calm and let your investments mature.

The Key Takeaway

Rain is temporary, and so are market storms. You don't need to rush or panic when things seem uncertain. Just like you wait for the rain to pass and the weather to clear, your investments will recover with time.

So, stay dry, stay steady, and trust in the long-term growth of your financial plan. Don't let a little rain dampen your spirits — or your portfolio.

18

Buy Trusted Brands – Not Every Stall Is Reliable

STICK TO KNOWN COMPANIES

Imagine buying rice from a vendor you've never seen before, just because it's ₹10 cheaper.

You get home, excited for a bargain, but when you open the bag — it's full of stones!

This is exactly what can happen in the stock market if you're not careful.

- **Unknown stocks** might seem like a good deal, but they lack the track record, trust, and stability that you need for long-term growth.
- Investing in an unknown company is like gambling with your money — you don't know if it will succeed, or if it will leave you empty-handed.

So, what should you do instead?

- **Stick to companies you understand**:
  These are brands you interact with every day. Think
  about companies like those in **FMCG, IT**, or
  banking sectors — names that have been around for
  years and have built a reputation you can trust.

- **Invest in companies you use and recognize**:
  You wouldn't buy a product from a brand you've
  never heard of. Similarly, when investing, make sure
  the company has a proven track record of success and
  stability.

- **If a company disappeared tomorrow, would
  you even notice?**
  Ask yourself: If a company suddenly shut down,
  would its absence make a noticeable difference in
  your life? If yes — it might be worth considering. But
  if not, then it may not be a smart investment.

In the market, just like in life, familiarity breeds trust. Stick
to companies that you're comfortable with and understand.

RESEARCH BEFORE YOU BUY

You wouldn't buy a ₹500 mango without checking it first, right?

Before you hand over that cash, you'll want to inspect it for:

- **Ripeness**: Is it too hard or too soft?
- **Smell**: Does it have that sweet fragrance, or is it off?
- **Seller's reputation**: Do you trust the vendor, or is there doubt?

The same principle applies before buying a stock:

- **What does the company do?**
  Understand the business model. Is the company in a growing sector? Does it align with future trends?
- **Is it profitable?**
  Check the company's earnings, debt, and profit margins. Just like ripe fruit, a profitable company is ready for the picking.
- **What's its past performance?**
  How has the company performed historically? While past performance doesn't guarantee future results, it gives you an idea of how resilient the company has been in both good and bad times.

You can find all of this information with the help of trusted financial tools like **Moneycontrol, Economic Times**, and mutual fund factsheets. These are your "fruit weighing scales" that help you assess whether the investment is ripe for picking or if it needs more time.

Remember, the time you spend researching now can save you from costly mistakes later.

The Key Takeaway:

A little research now equals a lot of savings later. Just as you wouldn't buy a mango without checking its quality, never buy a stock without doing your due diligence. Stick to what you know, and only invest in companies that make sense to you.

19

When to Change Vendors – Exit Bad Stocks

KNOWING WHEN TO SELL

Your vegetable vendor gave you stale spinach 3 times.

Would you still keep buying from him?

Just like that, some stocks stop performing. They may:

- Have poor results quarter after quarter
- Face legal issues or heavy debt
- Lose relevance due to new tech or trends

Signs it's time to sell:

- Company is no longer profitable
- You bought it on a tip, not research
- You need funds for an emergency
- Your investment goal has changed

*"Selling is not failure. It's **smart reshuffling** — like choosing fresher veggies."*

HOW TO REVIEW YOUR PORTFOLIO

Reviewing your stock basket is like checking your fridge once a week:

- Throw out what's gone bad
- Restock what's essential
- Try a new recipe if needed

Do this every:

- 3–6 months (portfolio check)
- Once a year (goal vs. investment match)
- Whenever your income or life situation changes

Use simple tools or apps to track:

- Growth of each stock
- Dividend earnings
- Sector diversification

Think of your portfolio as a **mini kitchen garden**:

- Needs water (regular investing)
- Needs pruning (selling bad stocks)
- Needs sunlight (knowledge and confidence)

TAKEAWAY!

Markets are part of life.

You don't need a finance degree — just your daily common sense.

The same care you use in running your home = care you need for managing your money.

> *"Because being financially independent isn't about earning crores...*
> *It's about knowing what to buy, when, and why*
> *— just like your daily shopping list."*

Part 8: Practice Before You Cook

So far, you've explored how to budget smartly, build your investment thali, manage your emotions, and even read the market like your daily kitchen.

Now, before diving in completely — let's do what every smart homemaker does: **practice before serving**.

Before any new dish reaches the family dinner table, what do we do?

☑ Try a small version

☑ Taste it

☑ Adjust the spices

That's exactly how investing works too.

Try. Taste. Tweak. Then Trust.

This part is your **trial kitchen** — your safe space to learn by doing without using real money.

You'll explore:

- **Paper trading** – practice investing with zero risk
- **Maintaining a simple diary** – track like you track groceries and expenses
- **Monthly reviews** – build confidence, one small step at a time

Because just like you don't serve a dish without tasting it, you don't need to invest real money before practicing.

Let's get comfortable, one spoon at a time — before the full feast!

20

Taste Before You Buy – Try Paper Trading

LEARN THROUGH SIMULATIONS

You wouldn't cook biryani for a wedding without testing the recipe first, right?

Similarly, **don't jump into the stock market without a practice round.**

Paper Trading = Simulated investing with no real money

You:

- Pick stocks
- Note down your "buy" price
- Track performance for 1–2 months
- See your "profit/loss" — **without risking a single rupee**

Use platforms like:

- Moneycontrol Portfolio Tracker
- TradingView Simulator
- Zerodha's Varsity Practice Tools

This is like doing a **mock run of your new dish** — so you learn what works, what burns, and what needs more salt.

MISTAKES YOU CAN LEARN FROM WITHOUT LOSING MONEY

Every beginner slips up. It's part of the learning curve.
Common first-timer mistakes include:

- Selling in panic or too early
- Buying stocks just because they're in the news
- Forgetting about hidden costs like taxes and brokerage fees

But here's the good news:
You can learn all of this — **without losing a single rupee**.

That's where **paper trading** (or virtual trading) comes in:

- You make real-time decisions using fake money
- You feel emotions like greed and fear
- You can try strategies without risk
- You build habits and gain confidence

It's like a dress rehearsal for your money journey.
No damage, just experience.

"Practice doesn't make perfect. It makes you prepared."

21

Maintain a Simple Investment Diary

TRACK LIKE HOUSEHOLD EXPENSES

Just like you track:
- Milk bills
- Monthly grocery spends
- Gas cylinder refills

You should also track:
- Which stock you bought
- When and why you bought it
- What your goal was
- How it's performing

Your investment diary doesn't have to be fancy. It can be:
- A notebook
- A Google Sheet
- A budgeting app like Walnut, Cube Wealth, or Excel

Include columns like:
- Stock name
- Buy price & date

- Reason for buying
- Goal (short-term, long-term, retirement)
- Review notes (every month)

REVIEW AND ADJUST EVERY MONTH

Like cleaning out your fridge:

- Check if something's expired
- See what's running low
- Plan meals accordingly

Your portfolio also needs:

- Regular **reviews** (what's working, what's not)
- Small **adjustments** (buy more of good stocks, sell weak ones)
- Periodic **top-ups** (reinvest dividends, increase SIPs)

Money grows with love + attention.

Set a monthly reminder: "Review My Investments – 1st of Every Month"

Make it as routine as:

- Grocery shopping
- Paying the school fees
- Filling the water cans

"A diary is not just about writing down...
It's about looking back and growing forward."

TAKEAWAY!

- ✓ Practice first. Like cooking a new recipe for the first time.
- ✓ Don't put your money into something you don't understand.
- ✓ Track every move, review every month — **like a true home CFO!**

"Money is not scary. It's just another ingredient.
Learn it. Taste it. Cook it your way."

Part 9: Speak the Market's Language – But Simple Style

You've learned how to budget like a homemaker, invest with balance, stay calm through market mood swings, and even shop the stock market like you do for your kitchen.
Now it's time to **speak the market's language** — in your own simple style!

Just like every kitchen has its own lingo — tadka, sabzi prep, masala base — the financial world has its own terms too. And no, they aren't scary once you hear them in your language!
In this part, we decode all those "complicated" money words using kitchen and bazaar talk.

Think of it like this:

- Stocks = shares in a shop
- IPO = grand opening
- Mutual Fund = your investment tiffin box
- Broker = your middleman uncle
- Demat = your digital locker
- Sensex = your market fitness score

Let's make the stock market feel like home — and start talking about money like it's your mother tongue.

22

Stock Market Made Simple

WHAT IS A STOCK?

A stock is simply a small piece of a company — like a spoon of biryani from a huge pot.

When you buy a stock, you're not just "putting money" somewhere. You're saying:
"I believe in this company. I want to own a part of it."

If the company does well — grows, earns more, becomes more valuable — your piece also increases in value.

Let's break it down:

- Suppose a company like Reliance is worth ₹1000 in total.
- It has 100 shares.
- That means each share is ₹10.
- If the company grows and becomes worth ₹2000, each share is now ₹20!

You didn't do anything extra — you just trusted the biryani to cook well, and now your spoonful is more delicious!

Stocks aren't lottery tickets — they're ownership tickets.

IPO = GRAND OPENING

IPO stands for **Initial Public Offering**.
That's just a fancy way of saying:
"We're opening our doors to the public — come invest in us!"

Imagine a brand-new shop opening in your area. The owners want to grow fast — so they invite you and others to contribute money, in exchange for a share of the profits.

Or better yet —
Think of it like a wedding invitation: "Come, celebrate with us, and contribute a gift (your money), and in return, we'll serve you a meal (shares) and make you a part of our future!"

People invest in IPOs because it's a chance to get in early.
But like any wedding food, some IPOs are spicy hits — others might give you a stomach ache.

So always read the **menu (prospectus)** before accepting the invite!

SHARES VS. EQUITY

These two terms often confuse people — but it's simple.

- **Equity** means ownership.
- **Shares** are the pieces or units that represent that ownership.

Imagine your favourite tiffin box:

- Equity is the **whole tiffin** — it's your full ownership of the meal.
- Shares are the **individual containers** — sabzi, dal, roti, sweet — each one represents a portion.

So, when someone says, "I hold equity in a company," they mean they have some level of ownership.

When they say, "I own 100 shares," they're talking about **how much** of that ownership they hold.

In short: **Equity is the concept. Shares are the quantity.**

23

Bull & Bear – Meet the Mood Swings of the Market

The stock market is emotional — just like us!

Some days it's cheerful and bursting with energy. Other days, it's moody, slow, and full of doubt.

It usually swings between two classic moods:

1.   Bull Market = Confidence & Growth

Think of a street full of aunties rushing to buy mangoes during the season.

There's excitement, high demand, prices shoot up — everyone wants a piece!

That's a **bull market** — the market is feeling confident, and prices of stocks keep rising.

Signs of a Bull Market:
- Positive news everywhere
- High investor confidence
- Companies doing well
- Stock prices climbing steadily

Your Action?

This is a good time to **invest more**, if your budget allows.

Build your portfolio while the market is smiling.

2. **Bear Market = Fear & Drop**

Now think of a week full of heavy rains — gloomy weather, roads flooded, veggies missing from the shelves.
Everyone stays home. No one wants to shop. That's a **bear market** — prices fall, and fear spreads.

Signs of a Bear Market:
- Negative headlines
- Low investor confidence
- Economic slowdown
- Stock prices dropping

Your Action?
Don't panic. **Stick to your plan. Review, don't react.**
Bear markets are part of the cycle — they pass, just like the rains.

Mood Matters — But Mindset Matters More.

The market will swing.
Your job is to stay steady — not swing with it.

"When others panic, stay calm. When others rush, think wisely."
Let the bulls and bears dance — you stay balanced.

24

Dividends, Mutual Funds & Brokers Explained Simple Style

MUTUAL FUND = INVESTMENT TIFFIN BOX

Think of a mutual fund like your daily lunch tiffin — neat, packed, and ready to eat. You don't cook it yourself, but you enjoy the meal.

In a mutual fund, **you give your money to a professional chef (called a fund manager).** This expert knows how to cook a healthy mix of investments.

Here's what they add to your financial tiffin:

- **Stocks (sabzis)** – some spicy, some plain, all meant to grow your money.
- **Bonds (roti)** – stable, filling, less spicy — they give steady returns.
- **Gold (sweet dish)** – maybe a bit fancy, but adds a safety touch.

The fund manager **stirs all of this together**, packs it nicely, and gives it back to you as a "mutual fund unit."

You don't have to worry about which share to buy, when to sell, or which stock is good. You just eat the tiffin (i.e., invest regularly) and let the chef handle the kitchen.

Great for beginners who want to start investing but don't know how to choose each ingredient individually.

BROKER = YOUR MIDDLEMAN

A broker is like your **friendly vegetable vendor uncle** at the local market.

You say, "Bhaiyya, get me 1 kg tomatoes and 2 kg onions," and he gets the best quality at the best price.
You don't run around the whole market — he does it for you.

In the stock world, a **stock broker** does the same thing.
You tell him, "I want to buy 10 shares of XYZ company," and he buys it for you from the stock market.

But there's one more thing you need — a **Demat account**.
It's like your shopping bag where all your stocks are kept safely in digital form. No paper, no hassle.

Some brokers are old-school like the uncles at sabzi mandi. Some are cool and modern — mobile apps where you tap and trade in seconds.They may charge a **small fee or commission**, just like the sabziwala adds ₹5 for carrying your bag — but they make your life easier.

DIVIDEND = BONUS LEMONS

Ever bought mangoes from a vendor and he says, "Madam, take these two lemons — free with love!"

That's exactly what **dividends** feel like.

When a company makes good profit, sometimes it shares a part of it with you — the shareholder. That's your reward for trusting them with your money.It's **not guaranteed**, but when it comes — it's a sweet surprise.
Some companies give dividends regularly, like your favourite vendor who always gives a little extra. Others reinvest the profits to grow more mangoes for later!
You can think of dividends as:
- **Mini bonuses**
- **Festival gifts**
- **Sweet thank-you notes** from the company

They don't make you rich overnight, but they surely make investing sweeter.

25

Demat, Nifty, Sensex & Portfolio Terms

YOUR DIGITAL LOCKER (DEMAT ACCOUNT)

No more paper share certificates.

A **Demat account** is like your **digital Tupperware box** – clean, organised, and safe.

It holds all your shares in digital form.

SENSEX = MARKET FITNESS SCORE

Sensex & Nifty are like:

- **Thermometers of the market**
- If they go up = market is healthy
- If they go down = fever alert!

Sensex = Top 30 companies

Nifty = Top 50 companies

Like a "topper list" of the school class.

26

Cheat Sheet – Market Terms in Kitchen & Street Lingo

Confused by terms like IPO, Bull Market, or Demat Account? Don't worry! Let's break them down with simple, everyday comparisons—because if you can shop smart, you can invest smart!

Stock Market Terms – Served Like a Home-Cooked Meal!

1. **Stock → One Slice of a Business Cake**

    - **What it means:** When you buy a stock, you own a tiny piece of a company—just like buying one slice from a whole cake.
    - **Why it matters:** If the company grows, your slice becomes more valuable!
    - **Example:** Buying ITC stock is like owning a small part of the biscuits and soaps you already use daily.

2. **IPO → A Grand Wedding Invite to Invest**

   - **What it means:** When a company goes public (IPO), it's like sending out invites—you get the first chance to invest before everyone else.
   - **Why it matters:** Early investors often get good prices, just like early wedding guests get the best seats!
   - **Example:** Imagine if Britannia had an IPO—you could've bought in early and grown your money with their biscuits!

3. **Equity → Your Total Tiffin Box**

   - **What it means:** Equity is your full ownership in a company—like all the compartments in your tiffin box.
   - **Why it matters:** More equity = bigger share in profits (and losses).
   - **Example:** If you own ITC, HUL, and Reliance stocks, your "tiffin box" has different flavors of investments!

4. **Mutual Fund → A Ready-Made Mixed Thali**

   - **What it means:** Instead of picking individual stocks (like cooking each dish), a mutual fund is a pre-mixed plate managed by experts.

- **Why it matters:** Less effort, more diversification—just like ordering a thali instead of cooking 5 separate dishes!

- **Example:** SIP in a mutual fund is like paying monthly for a chef to prepare your financial meals.

5. **Broker → Your Trusted Sabziwala (Stock Vendor)**

- **What it means:** A broker helps you buy/sell stocks, just like your sabziwala helps you pick the freshest veggies.

- **Why it matters:** A good broker saves you time and gets you the best deals.

- **Example:** Zerodha, Groww, and Upstox are like modern-day digital sabzi markets for stocks!

6. **Dividend → Free Curry Leaves or Lemons**

- **What it means:** Some companies share profits with shareholders—like getting free coriander leaves with your purchase.

- **Why it matters:** Extra income without selling your stocks!

- **Example:** If you own HUL shares, they might send you a "dividend" just for holding them.

7. **Demat Account → Your Airtight Dabba (Share Locker)**

- **What it means:** A digital locker where your stocks are stored safely—no papers, no theft risk.
- **Why it matters:** Just like you wouldn't leave cash lying around, never buy stocks without a Demat account!
- **Example:** Opening a Demat account is as essential as having a kitchen dabba for spices.

8. Bull Market → Mango Season Rush!

- **What it means:** When stock prices rise (like mangoes in summer), everyone wants to buy.
- **Why it matters:** Great time to invest—but don't overpay!
- **Example:** The 2020-21 stock boom was like a "mango season" for investors.

9. Bear Market → Rainy Week at the Market

- **What it means:** When prices fall, people panic (like vendors during monsoon when fewer customers come).
- **Why it matters:** Best time to buy "discounted" stocks—if you stay patient!

- **Example:** COVID crash was a "bear market," but those who bought low earned big later.

10. Sensex/Nifty → School Report Card of Top Companies

- **What it means:** Sensex (30 big companies) & Nifty (50 top companies) show if the market is passing or failing.
- **Why it matters:** If Sensex/Nifty grows, most stocks do well—just like good grades mean a bright future!
- **Example:** A rising Sensex = your investments are likely growing too.

11. Portfolio → Your Weekly Kitchen Menu

- **What it means:** Your mix of stocks, mutual funds, and other investments—like balancing dal, rice, and veggies.
- **Why it matters:** Diversification = less risk (don't put all money in just "one dish"!).
- **Example:** A smart portfolio has stocks (spices), mutual funds (curries), and bonds (rice)—all in the right proportion.

TAKEAWAY!

Every stock market term has a simple meaning.
Once you learn the lingo, **you stop feeling lost** and start
feeling **in charge**.
Speak the language of money with **kitchen confidence**.

> "If you can manage a kitchen, a family, a home –
> You can absolutely manage a portfolio, a
> budget, and a future."

Part 10: Tiny Habits, Big Wealth

You've explored your financial kitchen — from budgeting like a pro homemaker to building your investment thali, managing emotions, and understanding how the market works like your daily kitchen.

Now, let's turn to the secret ingredient that holds it all together: **tiny habits**.

Because just like adding a pinch of salt daily keeps your food tasty, small money habits — done every day — can quietly build lifelong wealth.

You don't need to make huge leaps. Just a simple 5-minute ritual, a quick check-in, or even visualizing your money goals can make a big difference over time.

This part is your guide to creating financial smarts that stick — not through pressure, but through practice.

Let's keep it light, simple, and doable — like adding that little pinch of salt every day to perfect your recipe.

27

One Daily Habit That Builds Financial Smarts

5-MINUTE DAILY RITUAL

Just like you make tea every morning ☐ — make **a 5-minute money ritual** part of your day.

Examples:

- Open your investment app — just look at it (no pressure to act).
- Check today's stock news headline.
- Read one personal finance tip or quote.
- Review your savings goal chart.
- Update your wallet spending.

☐ *Just 5 minutes — but it trains your brain to think money daily.*

DAILY TRACKER

Create a tiny "Money Habit Tracker" — like a kitchen chalkboard or notebook.

Make columns like:

- Checked stocks
- Read 1 tip
- Learnt 1 new term
- Saved ₹10+ today

Tick them daily. Even if you miss some, the tracker will keep you aware.

AFFIRMATIONS & VISUALS

Stick these on your mirror, fridge, or kitchen door:

- "I am learning to manage money like a pro."
- "Every rupee I save is self-respect in action."
- "My money works as hard as I do."

Visualise your dreams:

- A peaceful retirement
- Paying for your child's education
- Owning your own shop or home

"Dream boards aren't silly — they train your subconscious."

28

Why It Works – Brain Science Behind Tiny Habits

YOU GROW WITHOUT REALIZING

There's a secret ally in your money journey — **your brain**.

Neuroscience shows that your brain is like soft clay. It *loves* patterns and *adapts quickly* to small, repeated actions.

When you do something small and consistent:

- Your brain feels **safe** — no pressure, no fear
- It opens up — you're **more likely to try new things**
- Confidence slowly **replaces confusion**

That's the power of **tiny habits**.

It's exactly like learning to cook.
You didn't start by making a feast.
You began with boiling water or toasting bread.
One day, you find yourself making biryani from memory — and it feels easy.

The same thing happens with money.

Read a headline today. Understand your budget tomorrow. Soon, you're investing with confidence — without ever having read a finance textbook!

30-DAY PRACTICE CHALLENGE

Want proof? Try this for 30 days. Make your own **printable calendar** or **tracker chart** — colourful, fun, fridge-friendly.

Then, each day:

- Spend just **5 minutes** on a money habit (reading an article, checking prices, noting expenses)
- Track your win with a tick mark or emoji
- Write **1 line of reflection** — what did you learn or feel today?

Examples:

- "Checked my wallet. Realized I've been overspending on snacks."
- "Learned what an SIP is. It's simpler than I thought!"

At the end of 30 days — reward yourself:
Buy a book, enjoy a self-care treat, or get a small gold coin as a symbolic win.

It's not about the money — it's about **celebrating consistency.**

TAKEAWAY!

We often wait for big moments: a raise, a bonus, the "right time."
But **real growth happens daily**, in tiny, invisible steps.

"Building wealth isn't about doing BIG things one day. It's about doing TINY things every day."

Think of habits as water droplets.
One drop is nothing.
Over time — it becomes a river that shapes your financial future.

You don't need to be perfect.
You just need to show up, **daily**.

Motivation fades. But discipline builds a life.

So next time you open your money journal or track your spending — smile.

You're training your brain, shaping your mind-set, and rewriting your future.

Part 11: Your First Investment Recipe – A Step-by-Step Action Plan

Perfect! You've come a long way — from understanding the kitchen basics of budgeting and emergency funds, to preparing your investment thali, adding the right masalas of mind-set, and even navigating the daily market like your neighbourhood vendor.

Now, it's time to bring it all together.

Welcome to your **First Investment Recipe** — simple, clear, and completely doable.

Because knowing is good, but doing is divine.

This part is your kitchen-tested action plan — a step-by-step recipe designed to help you make your very first investment with confidence.

No guesswork. No confusion.

Just a clear, repeatable path to get started — with all the comfort and clarity of a well-loved home-cooked meal.

"A goal without a plan is just a wish."

Let's turn your money wish into a real dish!

Step 1: Pick Your Main Ingredient – Your Goal

What are you saving or investing for?

- Emergency fund
- Child's education

- Dream vacation
- A small business
- Retirement peace

Write it down. Put it on your fridge. This becomes your "main dish."

Step 2: Set the Cooking Time – Your Time Frame

How long do you have to reach that goal?

- 1 year?
- 5 years?
- 10+ years?

Short-term = use safer ingredients like Fixed Deposits or Liquid Mutual Funds.

Long-term = try stocks, SIPs, and balanced mutual funds.

Step 3: Chop It Down – Monthly Amount

Let's say your goal is ₹60,000 in 1 year.

Break it down: ₹5,000/month or ₹1,250/week.

This makes the dish easy to cook, bit by bit.

Step 4: Make Your First Grocery List – Open Accounts

Get your tools ready:

- Open a **Demat Account** (for stocks or mutual funds)
- Set up a **Savings Account** just for your goal

- Download 1-2 reliable apps (Zerodha, Groww, Kuvera etc.)

Like getting utensils before you cook.

Step 5: Choose Your Vegetables – Pick Investment Options

Based on your comfort level:

- Mutual Fund SIP (Start with ₹500/month)
- A Blue-Chip Stock (Like TCS, HUL, Infosys)
- Recurring Deposit (Safe & predictable)
- Gold Bonds (For long-term safety)

Start with 1–2 items only. Simpler = better.

Step 6: Taste Test – Track & Adjust Monthly

Once a month:

- Check your growth
- Adjust amounts if needed
- Celebrate small wins

Keep a **Money Diary** like your spice box — neat, daily, yours.

Step 7: Serve & Share – Involve Your Family

Let your spouse, kids or friends know:

- What you're saving for
- What you're learning
- How they can join too!

Money talk should be as normal as dinner talk.

Bonus Tip: Your Starter Plate

If you feel unsure, here's a simple **starter combo**:

Item	Amount	Type
Emergency Fund	₹1,000/month	Recurring Deposit
SIP	₹500/month	Balanced Mutual Fund
Gold	₹500/month	Gold ETF or Sovereign Gold Bond

- ✎ Total: ₹2,000/month
- ✎ Even this small step can lead to **lakhs in 5–10 years**!

FINAL THOUGHT!

Just like in the kitchen, you'll mess up some days.

Some stocks won't work out. Some savings will stop. Some days you'll feel lost.

But like every strong homemaker, **you'll bounce back, re-plan, re-cook, and grow.**

Because now… **you're not just managing a home. You're managing wealth.**

YOU DID IT!

You've completed a wholesome, desi-friendly, life-changing journey from: **Tomato prices to stock markets, kitchen jars to budgeting tools, daily cooking to daily investing.**

Now go ahead... **serve yourself your first bowl of financial freedom.**

READ THIS EVERY MORNING

A Wealth Manifesto for Women & Homemakers

I am a woman.

I don't just run a home —

I build dreams, manage time like magic, and stretch every rupee with care.

I turn small things into something meaningful — every single day.

I may not wear a suit or sit in boardrooms,

But I budget like a pro, plan like a leader,

And I **understand the value of money** deeply.

Now, it's **my time** to make **money work for me**.

I believe **money isn't just for the working world or for men** —it's for every woman who runs a home, runs a life, and keeps everything together.

I don't fear the stock market —
I see it as a **marketplace of opportunity**, full of fresh chances every day.
I don't need a fortune to begin —
I start small, stay consistent, and grow with confidence.
I don't chase quick returns —
I build **slow, steady, meaningful wealth**.
I don't follow the noise —
I pick my investments **just like fresh produce** — carefully and with love.
I don't wait for someone else to manage my money —
I trust myself, my learning, and my vision.
I don't invest just for profits —
I invest to **lead, grow, and inspire** — for myself, my family, and future generations.
I am not *just* a homemaker.
I am a **Household CFO, Budget Queen, and Smart Investor in Progress**.
Whether I wear an apron or heels,
Plan tiffin's or groceries —
I'm also learning to track stocks, build portfolios,
And grow money like herbs on my kitchen shelf.
I don't wait for the "right moment" —
I start **today**, one small step at a time.

I AM A WOMAN.

**And I am the CEO of my Financial Future.
My journey doesn't end in the kitchen — It
starts there, and leads me toward financial
freedom.**

Let this be your morning reminder.
Stick it on your wall. Read it out loud. Believe in it.
Because when a woman takes charge of her money — **She
takes charge of her future.**

ALL THE BEST

&

HAVE A WONDERFUL LIFE!

www.ingramcontent.com/pod-product-compliance
Lightning Source LLC
Chambersburg PA
CBHW031302130726
47988CB00007B/2683